# Gather Around Cocktails

# Gather Around Cocktails

DRINKS TO CELEBRATE USUAL
AND UNUSUAL HOLIDAYS

AARON GOLDFARB

DOVETAIL

Copyright © 2019 by Dovetail Press
Text by Aaron Goldfarb
Photographs by Scott Gordon Bleicher, except for page 16
Design by Limor Evenhaim

Published by Dovetail Press in Brooklyn, New York, a division of
Assembly Brands LLC.

For details or ordering information, contact the publisher at the address below or
email info@dovetail.press.

Dovetail Press
42 West Street #403
Brooklyn, NY 11222
www.dovetail.press

Library of Congress Cataloging-in-Publication data is on file with
the publisher.
ISBN: 978-1-7326952-2-1
First printing, September 2019
Printed in Turkey
10 9 8 7 6 5 4 3 2 1

Dedicated to the daughter of
a Christmas tree farmer who
taught this Jew to love eggnog.

# Contents

# Introduction

When you're a kid, there's nothing better than going to a party. You don't need much. A table covered with pizzas from a franchised chain, a few liters of Coke, a cake at the end, and maybe a gift bag to go. Now that's a party.

But wait, actually there's nothing better than going to a party when you're just coming of drinking age. Again, you don't need much. A space—whether a vacated house, a frat, *the woods*—sans adults, plus some alcohol. The quality of the latter is always irrelevant. If both sexes are there even better.

Now *that* is a party, man!

For most people, parties don't really get any better than that. You enter adulthood and all the so-called "festive" occasions start becoming things you'd rather try to get out of. ("I'll, uh, be . . . on jury duty . . . on . . . *Saturday*.") Compared to a bar, the alcohol selection at a party is almost always worse, compared to a restaurant, the food is too, and, at these adult parties, you actually have to converse with people you kinda know but kinda don't and would rather not. *All night long*.

How did we get to this point where we all dread parties?!

Watch movies and TV shows from the past, and adult cocktail parties look *wild*. Sloshing Manhattans and martinis and massive, heavily spiked punches. The record player is rocking and everyone is laughing and dancing and kissing and maybe someone even ends up passed out in the corner with a lampshade on their head at the end of the night.

The problem is, somewhere along the way—I'll say during the '90s—the consummate party hosts went from Hugh Hefner and Holly

Golightly types to modern-day Ward and June Cleavers out in the 'burbs. Today, at-home entertaining means inviting other respectable adults over for polite conversation, bland bites, and, worst of all, nothing too *strong*. Maybe a sangria which is essentially just fruit salad floating in wine. Or punches that are nothing more than store-brand lemonade with a splash of flavored vodka. Big vats of Cool Whip–heavy, whiskey-light, and always *pasteurized* eggnogs served out of ornate crystal bowls placed on the giant kitchen island in some indistinguishable McMansion. Think Martha Stewart or Ina Garten, who seem to care more about showing off their expensive glassware and dainty dishes than their mixology skills. Now, nothing against Martha or Ina (or even Ward and June Cleaver), but what hip person wants to attend one of their refined parties?

When I want to party, I want to party!

Then again, the only reason Martha and Ina got to define what "hosting" looks like in the 21st century is because today's young urbanites forgot how to throw real adult parties. Think about how many parties you've been to where the host considers a few six-packs of lite beer and a few bags of lime–flavored tortilla chips "festive" enough so long as "Jingle Bell Rock" is playing on Spotify and everyone is wearing an ironic ugly sweater?

Admittedly, many of today's twenty- and thirty-somethings lack the money and especially space that partiers from the past had. So do I, but I've never let that stop me from gathering friends under my roof.

You see, I long for a return to an earlier age—at least partying-wise—where hosts went all out during the holidays, preparing eggnogs and boozy punches and *cutting loose*. These days are slowly being revived, as both bartenders and home entertainers are starting to realize that seasonal and often large batch drinks aren't just mommy blogger stuff, but rather the key to celebrating any occasion.

Now I'm no Hugh Hefner (thank god), nor am I Holly Golightly—though I do like a danish—I'm just a Brooklyn husband and dad who likes to throw a great party. My apartment isn't massive and prepping stuff in my kitchen is a nightmare, especially if a second person enters the room, but I still love going all out for the holidays. And knowing just one solid cocktail for each event on the calendar will set you up for party success.

Eggnog is, of course, the quintessential winter holiday cocktail and in this book we'll start with it. I've come to realize so few drinkers have ever truly had it. Yeah, you've all had the quart of prepackaged Kroger's nog, but have you ever had the pleasure of a freshly beaten batch of the "real" stuff? Every December I host a holiday party at my home that we've taken to calling the Eggnog Social—I produce like five gallons worth—which has led to me becoming an expert on making this creamy, silky, boozy treat. You'll become an expert quicker than you think (so long as you have a stand mixer).

But the book also offers other cocktails for the chilly season. You'll learn how to make a Halloween-friendly, pumpkin-flavored punch that can actually be served inside a pumpkin. Thanksgiving gives us the opportunity to use the season's flavors in a big bowl of booze that will bring the whole family together, even your most politically argumentative relatives. There's a Hanukkah cocktail that tastes like a treat from the holiday—and, yes, you can drink it for eight straight nights. Other rich, creamy punches and hot, mulled drinks that are perfect for winter will make an appearance.

As the calendar turns over to a new year, the drinks will get a little more chill. A Groundhog Day cocktail that can be served hot or cold, depending on whether the little rodent sees his shadow or not. A Super Bowl Sunday cocktail you'll serve from a keg. A Valentine's Day drink you can garnish with loving phrases and symbols. Be Mine!

There's an Easter cocktail served inside a hollowed-out chocolate bunny. And an Oscars party one that comes in a popcorn box. Mardi Gras will give us the chance to turn the iconic King Cake into a cocktail too—the king baby will be hiding in ice cubes. Don't swallow it.

Summer party drinks will be great for cooling down; low-ABV sippers can be served on the patio or at a backyard BBQ all day long. There's a Memorial Day weekend drink that looks like a potted plant, and a Fourth of July punch that can be served inside a hollowed-out watermelon. There's a drink for Mother's Day and a less frilly one for daddy dearest.

This book will also have the perfect cocktails for some of life's greatest celebrations. Birthdays, weddings . . . there's a gender reveal party cocktail that will turn pink or blue depending on what's coming. Now share that pic on Facebook!

It's not just the major holidays either. If you learn anything from this book, you should learn that every "day" is an excuse to gather around. Leap Day gives us a rhubarb-based drink you can literally only have every four years. The Arbor Day drink will have us communicating with nature in liquid form.

All of these holidays necessitate having some friends over.

All of these call for a little celebration.

All of these deserve a truly festive cocktail.

Now *that's* a party!

# What You'll Need

This isn't the section from every cocktail book that spends pages telling you that you need to go buy a jigger and a stirrer. (Does every cookbook spend the first few chapters telling you to acquire some forks?) This section is more for party preparedness—how to knock it out of the park without spending too much money or time in the kitchen.

### A location

No, it doesn't need to be some multiroom mansion set in some cul-de-sac with full-time staff. A studio apartment is fine and will, in fact, probably be more fun. During the warmer months, any outdoor space can serve as a pretty perfect party location—a backyard, a rooftop, and even a parking lot, if tailgating's your thing.

### A way to invite people

This doesn't need to be formal either. Many people are so intimidated by the mere aspect of sending invites that they find it easier to just not have a party. But a party invite doesn't need to be formal. A free Paperless Post is fine, as is a Facebook invite. (Just make it private so the "friends" you don't invite don't learn about it.) Or an email! (Just be sure to BCC everyone.) Or, text a few key people if it's a small gathering. Who cares?! Let people know you're having a great party any way you can and *they will show up*!

A willingness to devote a little time to the cause

You can't just do a quick Swiffer and then lay out a handle of Bacardi and a few cans of ginger ale; for some of these cocktail recipes you will need to begin prepping a few days in advance. But it won't be grueling or laborious by any means. Many of the cocktails in this book are large format (i.e. punches)—meaning, you can pre-batch them in large quantities ahead of time so you won't have to make anything else during the party, and can actually enjoy yourself like any other party guest.

A decent punch bowl

You can use it as a serving vessel for most of the large format cocktails in this book, so having a good option or two is crucial.

# Syrups

Syrups are at the heart of almost every cocktail, and they can be as diverse as they are easy to make. The base is a simple combo of equal parts sugar and water, and the flavor additions are endless: from spices and herbs to fruits and nuts . . . you can pretty much make a syrup out of anything. This section includes the syrups you'll use in this book—they can and should be made ahead of time so your work during the party is minimal.

| | |
|---|---|
| Peppermint Syrup | 20 |
| Pistachio Syrup | 20 |
| Rhubarb Syrup | 21 |
| Spiced Cranberry Syrup | 21 |
| Toasted Pecan and Brown Sugar Syrup | 22 |
| Toffee Syrup | 22 |
| Winter Syrup | 23 |
| Yuengling Beer Syrup | 23 |

# Classic Simple Syrup

Makes 12 ounces

1 cup granulated sugar

1 cup water

In a small saucepan, combine the sugar and water and warm over medium heat until the sugar is fully dissolved. Remove from heat and cool to room temperature. Pour into a container and refrigerate until ready to use or up to 2 weeks.

# Charoseth Syrup

⅔ cup honey

1 cup water

1 apple, finely chopped

½ cup walnuts, crushed

In a small saucepan, combine the honey and water and warm over medium heat until fully combined. Remove from heat and add the apple and walnuts. Let sit for 1 hour then strain into a container and refrigerate until ready to use or up to 2 weeks.

# Christmas Tree Syrup

A handful of pine needles

1 cup granulated sugar

1 cup water

Pluck the freshest, greenest needles from your Christmas tree, wash, then chop them. (To make sure your pine tree isn't toxic, see page 46.)

In a small saucepan, combine the sugar and water and warm over medium heat until the sugar is fully dissolved. Remove from heat and add the pine needles. Let sit for a few hours to allow the pine needles to infuse the syrup. Strain into a container and refrigerate until ready to use or up to 2 weeks.

# Cinnamon Syrup

1 cup granulated sugar

1 cup water

3 to 4 cinnamon sticks

In a small saucepan, combine the sugar, water, and cinnamon sticks, and warm over medium heat until the sugar is fully dissolved. Remove from heat and let sit for a few hours to allow the cinnamon sticks to infuse the syrup. Strain into a container and refrigerate until ready to use or up to 2 weeks.

# Demerara Syrup

1 cup demerara sugar

1 cup water

In a small saucepan, combine the sugar and water and warm over medium heat until the sugar is fully dissolved. Remove from heat and cool to room temperature. Pour into a container and refrigerate until ready to use or up to 2 weeks.

# Ginger Syrup

1 cup granulated sugar

1 cup water

1 cup sliced ginger

In a small saucepan, combine the sugar and water and warm over medium heat until the sugar is fully dissolved. Remove from heat and add the ginger. Let sit for a few hours to allow the ginger to infuse the syrup (the longer it sits, the more gingery it will be). Strain into a container and refrigerate until ready to use or up to 2 weeks.

# Gingerbread Syrup

1 cup granulated sugar

1 cup water

1 tablespoon ground cinnamon

1 teaspoon ground nutmeg

½ teaspoon vanilla extract

2 tablespoons grated ginger

In a small saucepan, combine the sugar, water, cinnamon, nutmeg, and vanilla, and warm over medium heat until the sugar is fully dissolved. Remove from heat and add the ginger, then let sit for a few hours to allow the ginger to infuse the syrup. Strain into a container and refrigerate until ready to use or up to 2 weeks.

# Grenadine

Makes 12 ounces

1 cup granulated sugar

1 cup pomegranate juice

In a small saucepan, combine the sugar and pomegranate juice and warm over medium heat until the sugar is fully dissolved. Remove from heat and cool to room temperature. Pour into a container and refrigerate until ready to use or up to 2 weeks.

---

# Lemongrass Syrup

Makes 12 ounces

1 cup granulated sugar

1 cup water

2 lemongrass stalks, finely sliced

In a small saucepan, combine the sugar and water and warm over medium heat until the sugar is fully dissolved. Remove from heat and add the lemongrass. Let sit for a few hours to allow the lemongrass to infuse the syrup. Strain into a container and refrigerate until ready to use or up to 2 weeks.

---

# Marshmallow Syrup

Makes 16 to 20 ounces

1 cup granulated sugar

1 cup water

8 large marshmallows

In a small saucepan, combine the sugar and water and warm over medium heat until the sugar is fully dissolved. Add the marshmallows and stir until they are fully dissolved. Let sit for a few hours to allow the lemongrass to infuse the syrup. Pour into a container and refrigerate until ready to use or up to 2 weeks.

# Mint Syrup

1 cup granulated sugar

1 cup water

A handful of mint leaves

In a small saucepan, combine the sugar and water and warm over medium heat until the sugar is fully dissolved. Remove from heat and add the mint leaves. Let sit for a few hours to allow the mint to infuse the syrup (the longer it sits, the more minty it will be). Strain into a container and refrigerate until ready to use or up to 2 weeks.

# Peppermint Syrup

Makes 12 to 16 ounces

1 cup water

12 candy canes, broken into pieces

In a small saucepan, combine the water and candy canes and warm over medium heat until the candy canes are fully dissolved. Remove from heat and cool to room temperature. Pour into a container and refrigerate until ready to use or up to 2 weeks.

# Pistachio Syrup

Makes 12 ounces

1 cup shelled, unsalted pistachios

1 cup water

1 cup granulated sugar

Soak the pistachios in the water for 30 minutes, then pour into a blender and blend until smooth. Let sit for 2 hours then strain into a saucepan using a cheesecloth. Add the sugar and warm over medium heat until the sugar is fully dissolved. Remove from heat and cool to room temperature. Pour into a container and refrigerate until ready to use or up to 2 weeks.

# Rhubarb Syrup

*Makes 8 to 10 ounces*

½ pound rhubarb stalks, sliced

1 cup granulated sugar

1 cup water

Strawberries (optional)

Preheat the oven to 350°F. In a baking dish, combine the rhubarb, sugar, and water. If you prefer a sweeter syrup that's more juicy and vibrant, add a handful of strawberries. Place in the oven and bake for 1 hour, stirring every 15 minutes. Strain into a container and refrigerate until ready to use or up to 2 weeks.

# Spiced Cranberry Syrup

*Makes 30 to 40 ounces*

2 cups cranberries (fresh or frozen)

1 cup granulated sugar

1 cup dry white wine

1 cup water

2 cinnamon sticks

Juice and peel of 1 orange

1 vanilla bean, split

1 star anise

Place the cranberries in a saucepan and cook over medium heat until they are soft, about 10 minutes. Add the sugar, wine, and water, and cook just below a simmer, until everything is combined. Remove from heat and add the cinnamon sticks, orange juice and peel, vanilla bean, and star anise. Stir together and let cool to room temperature. Strain into a container and refrigerate until ready to use or up to 2 weeks.

# Toasted Pecan and Brown Sugar Syrup

Makes 12 ounces

½ cup pecans

1 cup brown sugar

1 cup water

Preheat the oven to 350°F. Place the pecans on a sheet pan and toast until you can smell them, about 5 minutes. In a small saucepan, combine the sugar, water, and the pecans, and bring to a boil. Cook for 10 to 15 minutes, then remove from heat and let cool to room temperature. Strain into a container and refrigerate until ready to use or up to 2 weeks.

# Toffee Syrup

Makes 16 to 20 ounces

1 cup granulated sugar

1 cup water

¾ cup crushed toffee pieces

In a small saucepan, combine the sugar, water, and toffee and warm over medium heat until the sugar and toffee are fully dissolved. Remove from heat and cool to room temperature. Pour into a container and refrigerate until ready to use or up to 2 weeks.

# Winter Syrup

Makes 100 ounces

8 cups granulated sugar

8 cups water

8 cinnamon sticks

8 star anise

8 cloves

8 whole nutmegs

2 vanilla beans

Zest of 1 orange

In a small saucepan, combine the sugar and water and warm over medium heat until the sugar is fully dissolved. Remove from heat and add the cinnamon, star anise, cloves, nutmegs, vanilla beans, and orange zest. Let sit for 2 hours to allow the spices to infuse the syrup. Strain into a container and refrigerate until ready to use or up to 2 weeks.

---

# Yuengling Beer Syrup

Makes 16 ounces

1 (12-ounce) bottle
Yuengling beer

1 cup demerara sugar

Pour the beer into a saucepan and simmer until it's slightly reduced. Add the sugar and stir until it is fully dissolved. Remove from heat and pour into a container and refrigerate until ready to use or up to 3 months.

# Winter Cocktails

**W**inter is a time of gathering indoors, out of the bitter cold, and that means the season's cocktails will tend to be for a large, chilly group, and designed for warming everybody up. These holiday drinks will often be rich, thick, creamy, spiced, and most definitely boozy.

Think hot toddies, mulled punches, and, of course, nogs (both with and without eggs, from America and from abroad). New Year's Eve will bring Champagne cocktails and unique ways to consume them, while New Year's Day will see us trying to start off our year of drinking a little more healthfully. And wait till you try the Valentine's Day cocktail—a decadent drink for the senses.

# Homemade Eggnog

Eggnog is the quintessential Christmas cocktail. Unfortunately, more so than perhaps any other cocktail, eggnog has been bastardized beyond all recognition. Even in this highly artisanal, DIY era, people are just not making their own nog often enough—instead, they simply buy a quart at the store and spike it themselves. Sad.

Fresh eggnog is easier to make than you'd think, far more delicious than seems possible, and incredibly impressive when served to a crowd. It will be a little messy however. You're also going to need a giant bowl—a gorgeous punch bowl preferably—but you could probably use a Dutch oven or a lobster pot in a pinch.

My eggnog is fairly traditional, other than the fact that I use three different alcohols for added complexity. So long as you know the basic ingredients and techniques, this eggnog is easy to fine-tune to your preferences.

12 eggs

6 cups whole milk

3 cups heavy cream

1 cup granulated sugar

6 ounces bourbon
(opt for a sweeter one
like Maker's Mark)

6 ounces dark rum
(but not "spiced" like
Captain Morgan)

6 ounces cognac or
apple brandy

Whole nutmeg,
for garnish

Separate the yolks from the egg whites. In a stand mixer, beat the whites on high speed until transformed into a fluffy meringue-like consistency with soft peaks.

Meanwhile, in a separate large bowl, whisk the yolks with the milk, cream, sugar, bourbon, rum, and cognac, until you get a smooth texture. Transfer the mixture to a large serving bowl, like a punch bowl or a Dutch oven. Gently fold in the beaten whites until just combined. Taste to make sure you're happy with the sweetness and booziness and tweak as needed. Chill it for a bit in the fridge before serving.

To serve, ladle a few ounces into a festive mug or glass, and using a microplane, grate fresh nutmeg over each serving.

# Single-Serving Eggnog

Admittedly, it's a lot of work to throw a party just so you can enjoy some eggnog. Thus, for the lazy nog lovers among us, knowing how to make single-serving nog is critical.

2 tablespoons granulated sugar

1 egg

2 to 3 ounces bourbon, rum, or cognac

½ cup whole milk or heavy cream

Whole nutmeg, for garnish

In a cocktail shaker, combine all the ingredients with ½ cup of ice. Shake for 20 to 30 seconds until frothy.

Strain into a glass, and using a microplane, grate fresh nutmeg on top.

# Aged Eggnog

Sitting in the back of my fridge, behind the jar of pickled jalapeños and a bottle of rosé my wife opened last summer but never finished, is a 64-ounce beer growler full of something older than my young daughter: an eggnog I first made over three years ago. Has it turned green and moldy? Is it straight milky poison? Hardly. Not only is it still drinkable, it's probably more delicious and safe than the fresh eggnog I'll make this year.

Believe it or not, people have been aging eggnog since colonial times. They didn't need the FDA or the National Egg Board to realize that booze sterilizes this eggy, creamy concoction, and allows it to keep indefinitely. Though I refrigerate mine, you don't have to—Manhattan bartender Nicolas Bennett stores his aging eggnog in a cool cupboard.

But how does it taste? Simply put: incredible. Any sort of alcoholic burn completely smooths out, as does the thick, frothy, sometimes chunky texture. What you're eventually left with is a nog smooth as silk, with a taste like a liquidized Werther's Original candy. I've found that about two to three weeks produces the best flavor and texture, but every year, at the end of my holiday party, I put any eggnog that wasn't consumed in a growler, toss it in the back of my fridge, and let time go to work.

# Flavored Nog

Eggnog is eggnog and it's delicious enough as is, there's really no reason to adulterate it. But I do understand wanting to have your eggnog stand out from the crowd. Thus, if you have any desire to make some sort of eggnog variant, what I recommend is you make the Homemade Eggnog (page 28) as a base, and then make a series of flavored syrups that party guests can mix in like they're working the frap counter at a Starbucks. Here are some suggestions for dressing up your eggnog.

- Gingerbread Syrup (page 18) with ginger snap garnishes

- Peppermint Syrup (page 20) with cracked candy cane "rims"

- Pistachio Syrup (page 20) with crushed pistachios on top

- Toffee Syrup (page 22) with toffee crumbles on top

# Nog in Other Countries

Your Eggnog Social need not be a strictly Americentric affair. Whether your guests are from diverse backgrounds, or simply interested in exploring other cultures' boozy egg customs, there's a variety of nog-like drinks that you could also consider hosting a holiday party around. (Or bottling to give as gifts.) For most of the nogs in this section you will only need to adulterate the Homemade Eggnog base (page 28).

### COQUITO

Puerto Rico's traditional winter drink means "little coconut" in Spanish and completely lacks eggs. Nevertheless, it remains nog-like due to its combination of coconut milk, coconut cream, sweetened condensed milk, and, of course, booze (usually rum).

### PONCHE CREMA

Venezuela's eggnog is likewise eggless, and often calls for an entire box of flan mix to be combined with whole milk, sweetened condensed milk, and rum.

### ROMPOPE

Served in Mexico and other parts of Latin America (such as Honduras, Costa Rica, and Nicaragua), this nog includes the standard ingredients of egg yolks, milk, sugar, and rum, with most people adding cinnamon sticks, vanilla extract, and even ground nuts like almonds or pecans as well. It is served either warm or chilled over ice.

### COLA DE MONO

This Chilean specialty (which translates to "monkey's tail") takes the national spirit of pisco and combines it with coffee and milk.

### TAMAGOZAKE

While more typically seen as a cold remedy in Japan, this intriguing combination of raw egg and sugar whisked into hot sake works great as a bit of a nog/hot toddy hybrid.

### EIERPUNSCH/ ADVOCAAT

This pasty egg elixir is often said to be so thick you could eat it with a spoon, but it remains popular in Germany and the Netherlands, especially in the countries' border towns. The warm drink is made with the expected egg yolks and sugar, though brandy, white wine, or even beer is often swapped in as the alcoholic component.

### AULD MAN'S MILK

Scots pound this smoky nog during their epic New Year's Eve celebration known as Hogmanay, which can often turn into a two-day bender. The name is, of course, meant to evoke Auld Lang Syne (penned by native son Robert Burns), and the drink combines eggs and sweetened cream with, you guessed it, scotch.

### MELKTERTJIES

This South African nog is served as a shooter and said to taste like *melktert*, a tart-like pastry popular in the country. Vodka is combined with condensed milk, cream, and a healthy dose of cinnamon.

# Spiced Mexican Chocolate Nog

Maybe you live where I live: in a cool urban environment filled with plant-based health nuts. Forget gluten and dairy, and get that cage-raised egg outta my face. Luckily, Jason Eisner, back when he was beverage director at Gracias Madre, a vegan Mexican restaurant in West Hollywood, created not just one, but two vegan nog analogs. Both of which his publicist at the time told me tasted "Very LA."

2 ounces unsweetened whole coconut milk

1½ ounces Xicaru Mezcal Espadin

½ ounce organic agave nectar

2 dashes chocolate bitters

1 pinch of Masala Chai tea blend

Organic cocoa powder, for garnish

Combine the coconut milk, mezcal, agave nectar, bitters, and Masala Chai tea blend in a shaker (without ice) and do a dry shake. Add ice and shake hard.

Strain into a coupe. Dust the top with some cocoa powder before serving.

# Eggless Avocado Nog

Another variation of egg(less) nog, which Eisner calls Abuelita's Champurrado, uses avocado to create the luscious, creamy texture expected in a nog. Easy to prepare in bulk ahead of time, it's perfect for a vegan holiday gathering.

²/₃ cup almonds

1½ cups granulated sugar

5 cups unsweetened whole coconut milk

1 cup vanilla hazelnut milk

2 cinnamon sticks

1 lemon rind, pith removed

1 teaspoon pure vanilla extract

¼ teaspoon baking soda

Flesh of ½ avocado

6 ounces blanco tequila

2 ounces mezcal

In a food processor, combine the almonds and 2 tablespoons of the sugar. Pulse on medium speed until the ingredients are ground into a fine paste.

In a large saucepan, combine the coconut milk, vanilla hazelnut milk, cinnamon sticks, lemon rind, vanilla, and baking soda and bring to a boil over medium-high heat. Reduce the heat and simmer for 15 to 20 minutes. Remove from heat, discard the cinnamon sticks and lemon rind, and let cool. Mash the avocado and whisk into the coconut/almond milk mixture, then add the ground almond paste and the remaining sugar. Return the saucepan to the stove and cook over low heat, constantly stirring and scraping the bottom and sides of the pan, until the mixture thickens enough to coat the back of a spoon, about 5 to 7 minutes. Remove from heat and let cool completely, about 2 hours.

Pour into a pitcher and stir in the tequila and mezcal. Serve in highball glasses.

*Pictured on page 35*

# Tom & Jerry

"Large format" cocktails are obviously perfect for parties. They allow you, as host, to do more important things than making drinks. But there is one large format drink where it would probably be better if you man the serving station all night.

This one is essentially a Wisconsified eggnog (the one place it is still ubiquitous today), but it was actually invented in Britain in the early 19th century. The cocktail is built piecemeal, with an eggnog-like batter (you can prepare beforehand) being added to a mug, followed by a healthy splash of booze, then hot milk from the stove.

Be sure not to leave your guests to their own devices when it comes to assembling their individual drinks. I once made the mistake of leaving the Tom & Jerry station unattended at my Christmas party, and later realized the guests had simply been drinking the high-calorie, non-alcoholic batter.

12 eggs

4 cups granulated sugar

2 tablespoons pure vanilla extract

1 teaspoon ground cinnamon

1 teaspoon ground allspice

1 teaspoon ground cloves

¾ gallon whole milk

2 cups cognac or brandy

2 cups aged rum

Whole nutmeg, for garnish

Separate the yolks from the egg whites, reserving the yolks in a separate bowl. In a stand mixer, beat the whites to soft peaks. Add the sugar to the yolks and whisk together. Gently fold the egg whites into the yolks until a batter forms. Stir in the vanilla, cinnamon, allspice, and cloves.

In a large saucepan, warm the milk on very low heat. To assemble individual drinks, pour 2 ounces of the batter into a mug, then stir in 1 ounce each of cognac and rum. Top with 6 ounces hot milk and stir until frothy. Using a microplane, grate fresh nutmeg on top.

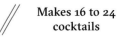

# Mexican Mulled Punch (Ponche Navideño)

Just like eggnog, almost every country has their own version of a mulled beverage. Whether *Glühwein* in Germany, *glögg* in Scandinavia, *vin brulé* in Italy, or *wassail* in the U.K., these hot, spiced drinks are quintessential winter warmers.

For a cozy winter holiday gathering, consider making this Mexican mulled punch traditionally served during Las Posadas, the nine-day celebration that culminates on Christmas Eve.

5 cinnamon sticks

20 cloves

8 ounces dried hibiscus flowers (wrapped in cheesecloth like a teabag)

1 tablespoon tamarind paste

2 (16-ounce) cans tejocotes

2 apples, chopped

2 pears, chopped

1 (30-ounce) can whole guava, chopped

¾ cup prunes, chopped

½ cup raisins

2 (8-ounce) cones of piloncillo (brown sugar cane) or 2 cups brown sugar

4 sugar cane sticks, cut into quarters

3 cups brandy, tequila, or rum

Orange or lemon slices, for garnish

In a large pot, combine the cinnamon sticks, cloves, hibiscus flowers, tamarind paste, and tejocotes with a gallon of water and bring to a boil. Reduce the heat to a simmer and add the apples, pears, guava, prunes, raisins, piloncillo, and sugar cane sticks Simmer for at least 30 minutes, stirring frequently until the fruit is soft and everything has combined. Remove the cinnamon sticks, cloves, and dried hibiscus flowers and discard. Add the alcohol and stir. Keep the pot on low heat so the punch stays warm for serving.

Serve in heat-resistant mugs, making sure each serving gets some fruit. Garnish with a slice of orange or lemon.

*Pictured on page 24*

# Learn to Mull, Win the Holidays

It's easy to mull whatever you want, whether with wine, cider, or beer, as long as you understand the basic concept of mulling.

So what is mulling? Well, it simply involves infusing so-called mulling spices into alcohol. Mulling spices are a know-'em-when-ya-see-'em thing. Cinnamon sticks, cloves, allspice, sure. Star anise and maybe ginger too. Pretty much anything that would be in that jar of potpourri on the back of grandma's toilet lid. Dried fruits like raisins, and lemon or orange peels work too.

It's not particularly hard to wing it. Just pick an alcoholic base (red wine and cider are most common, beer less so, spiking it even more with aquavit is kinda cool), toss in some sugar or a sweetener like honey, and then throw in your mulling spices and heat it all up. You can use a large saucepan, though a Dutch oven works even better. I sometimes use an electronic slow-cooker which allows me to keep the mulled wine hot and mulling all night long.

# Jelly Doughnut Beertail

While Christmas is rife with cocktail standards, us Jews don't really get any for our holiday season. Which is absurd, because we have eight different nights to have people over to light the menorah and celebrate! Yeah, I suppose you could make an eggnog with rabbi-blessed eggs and Manischewitz, but I mean come on.

"I can think of one very obvious reason Hanukkah has no cocktail," jokes Chaim Dauermann, the co-owner of New York's Stay Gold and bar director at The Up & Up, not to mention a practicing Jew. "Because it's a *children's* holiday."

Of course, he's right, but even so, he decided to turn one of the Festival of Lights' most iconic bites into this boozy sip (which he calls Bread & Oil). While re-creating a latke was the obvious call—more on that in a second—this is meant to channel sufganiyot. These small, jelly-filled, black currant–tasting, oil-fried doughnuts are enjoyed to help us recall the holiday miracle when a small lamp of oil burned for eight days instead of the expected one.

Similarly, unlike one-day-only Christmas libations, you and your guests can drink this cocktail for eight straight nights.

1 cup Glenmorangie

6 ounces crème de cassis

4 ounces Classic Simple Syrup (page 16)

2 ounces fresh lemon juice

2 (12-ounce) bottles brown ale

Lemon slices, for garnish

In a pitcher, pre-batch by combining the scotch, créme de cassis, syrup, and lemon juice, and stir.

To serve, pour 2½ ounces of the batch into individual glasses filled with ice, then top with the brown ale. Garnish with slices of lemon.

# The Liquid Latke

If potato latkes are the most famous dish associated with Hanukkah, it would make sense to try and recreate a drinkable version of them—a seemingly easy task as vodka is often made from potatoes. Dauermann takes potato vodka, apple brandy (to simulate the applesauce often used for dipping), and milk (to simulate sour cream) and then clarifies the mixture. Clarifying is an esoteric though old-fashioned process hip with bartenders these days, that causes the milk to curdle and then strips the color from the liquid after a few hours of straining.

"Sometimes my cocktails tend to be very narrative," Dauermann explains. "With this one I really wanted to be able to relate the miracle of clarification with the miracle in the story of Hanukkah." Dauermann claims only the most dedicated cocktail nerd should even attempt to make it, as he admits it's not necessarily the tastiest drink.

# The Rum Fire Shots Menorah

No menorah? No problem! Use booze and shot glasses instead. Gather eight shot glasses of uniform height plus one shot glass that's a little taller than the rest and line them up like a menorah (they also sell shot glass menorahs on Etsy). Fill the glasses with overproof alcohol—anything over 80 proof should light, but the higher the proof the easier it will flame—like Booker's Bourbon, Wray & Nephew, or my personal favorite, Rum Fire. Light the booze candles and let them burn as long as you'd like. It should take a good two to three hours for the liquor to completely burn off. Or, you can just blow them out almost instantly and, along with eight other guests, chug the shots. Happy Hanukkah, indeed.

# Pine Needle Punch

The five days between Christmas and New Year's Eve are kinda boring and always make me feel a little antsy, especially if I've been stuck in a home with the same people, animals, and leftovers for too many days in a row. The stress and impending doom is even worse if you still have that Christmas tree lingering in the corner of the living room, slowly dying, just begging you to end its month of misery.

Here's what you should do to cheer yourself up: invite your friends over for a party. They can do the Christmas tree removal work while you make them a celebratory drink. In this martini-like punch, gin supercharges the piney botanical notes from the pine needles, which you'll pull from your Christmas tree and use in an aromatic syrup. (To make sure your pine tree isn't toxic, see page 46.) Another fun, attractive hack is to use frozen cranberries (or other frozen fruits) instead of ice. As the cranberries warm up they will add new flavors to the punch.

3 cups gin or vodka

1½ cups dry vermouth

1½ cups Christmas Tree Syrup (page 17)

6 ounces fresh lemon juice

1 (12-ounce) package frozen cranberries (optional)

1 (750-milliliter) bottle Champagne or sparkling wine

Pine needles, for garnish

In a large punch bowl, combine the gin, vermouth, syrup, and lemon juice, then add a giant ice cube (see page 124) or frozen cranberries. Top with the Champagne.

The guests can serve themselves and garnish their drinks with a few pine needles.

# A Brief Note on the Safety of Drinking Christmas Trees

All Christmas trees aren't edible, no surprise. Organic ones are typically good, spruce or Douglas fir especially. On the other hand, ponderosa pine, yew, and hemlock are poisonous when ingested, and you should know that about hemlock if you've ever read about Socrates. If you want to be cautious, you can call the farm where you got the tree and see if they use weapons-grade pesticides on their trees (that's no good). Finally, pregnant women and children shouldn't drink anything made with pine needles, or probably booze either.

# French 750

New Year's Eve parties have a particular lifespan for humans. When you're a kid you're happy if you're allowed to stay up till midnight. When you're young and of legal age, you go to bars that have "all-you-can-drink" specials but are so packed it is literally impossible to drink-all-you-can. Eventually, you get a little older, a little wiser, a little less eager to go out among all the other ball-drop enthusiasts. So you invite other "adults" to your house to drink something bubbly, elegant, and *expensive*—a perfect way to count down to next year. You enjoy some French 750s (yes, 750s, we're using full 750-milliliter bottles here) and by the end of the night you realize you're not as grown-up as you thought.

Many will debate whether this quintessential, pre-prohibition Champagne cocktail should be made with gin or cognac, but the latter feels a whole lot more elegant for the big night.

1 (750-milliliter) bottle cognac

6 ounces fresh lemon juice

4 ounces Classic Simple Syrup (page 16)

2 (750-milliliter) bottles dry Champagne, chilled

Long lemon peel twists, for garnish

In a large pitcher or a punch bowl, pre-batch by combining the cognac, lemon juice, syrup, and 1¼ cups water, and chill for at least an hour. Keep the Champagne chilled until party time.

To make individual drinks, pour about 3 ounces of the batch into a large coupe, and top with 3 ounces of Champagne. Garnish with a lemon twist.

# Flute or Coupe?

Ah, the eternal Champagne debate—to serve it in a flute or a coupe? Now, admittedly, most people don't own the latter, while most own a few of the former. Unfortunately, until recently, not many home goods stores at the mall sold coupes. Still, there has to be a better reason why the flute became the ubiquitous way to drink Champagne. It is said that flutes help with the nucleation of the Champagne's bubbles and so they won't dissipate too quickly. *Sure.* But they don't hold much liquid (re-pour after re-pour), so I always opt for the coupe. It's a tad more, uh, sloshy, but it's way more elegant. And, more importantly, much better for building Champagne towers.

# Instagrammable Champagne Silliness

Drink enough French 750s and the party can really get started. Just make sure your friends have their phones out to take pics and tag you on social media. (Your boss doesn't follow you, does she?) Here are a few fun New Year's Eve stunts that look great for the camera, in order of difficulty.

---

### DRINKING FROM A HIGH HEEL

Drinking from a woman's "slipper", a practice that first started in Belle Époque Paris, became a symbol of joyful decadence and depravity in turn-of-the-century America. Of course, no one has really done this since Tallulah Bankhead was still on the Hollywood A-list . . . but there's no reason not to revive the practice. Just ask for permission first. And make sure there are backup pairs of shoes available so your guests can walk home.

## SABERING A BOTTLE

Just as badass as it looks, sabering a bottle of bubbly is actually a whole lot easier than you'd think. You don't need some crazy cavalry sword—a butter knife will work fine. Make sure your Champagne bottle is thoroughly chilled. (And make sure no one is standing in front of you!) Remove the foil and wire cage. Find the seam running up the glass and use that as your saber runway. Hold the blunt edge of your saber on the seam—most people mess up by thinking it's the sharpness of the knife that does the work—and then strike upward and away from you, toward the bottle's lip. If done correctly, the cork and a ring of glass should dislodge. Enjoy glasses of champers. Swiffer the floor.

---

## POURING A CHAMPAGNE TOWER

Talk about wasteful and potentially messy! But if you pull this off, people will think you're greater than Gatsby. You'll need at least 30 coupes and an incredibly sturdy table. Start by building square bases of coupes on top of one another—the bottom level of 4-by-4 coupes, then 3-by-3 on top of that, then 2-by-2, leading up to 1 coupe on top. (All the glasses should be tightly touching one another, creating a diamond shape between them.) Slowly pour Champagne into the top glass until it starts overflowing and trickling to each layer below it. Now is not the time to be a chicken and use the cheap stuff, though it will take around six bottles to fill this tower. Once all the glasses are filled, serve guests from the top and enjoy your round of applause.

# Bloody Mary Bar

Good morning and welcome to the New Year. Maybe you had a late one last night, drinking the bubbly out of a random lady's high heel (was that not your wife?!), sabering bottles of Dom, and then pouring it down a Champagne tower of your own construction. You might want to sit today out.

But . . . maybe you retired well before the ball dropped and actually got a good night's rest, waking up refreshed and ready to tackle the new year. Nothing wrong with that. We can make up for the partying we missed last night today. Because, increasingly, more and more people are opting to only have New Year's *Day* parties. It doesn't have to be a lot of work, and since you're hosting it, you won't even have to leave your house (or put on shoes) till January 2.

This self-serve, make-your-friends-do-all-the-work Bloody Mary Bar is meant for today. You'll make red and green Bloody bases in the morning—your guests will do the rest of the work once they start arriving around midday.

FOR THE RED
BLOODY BASE:

24 heirloom tomatoes

1 cup fresh lime juice

6 tablespoons chopped
fresh cilantro

2 jalapeños, seeded

3 tablespoons horseradish

1 teaspoon ground cumin

1 teaspoon smoked paprika

FOR THE GREEN
BLOODY BASE:

30 tomatillos, husks removed

18 yellow tomatoes

1 cup fresh lime juice

6 tablespoons chopped
fresh cilantro

2 jalapeños, seeded

3 tablespoons horseradish

1 teaspoon ground cumin

1 teaspoon smoked paprika

FOR THE BLOODY
SELF-SERVE STATION:

2 (750-milliliter) bottles
vodka or spirit of choice

Your choice of garnishes,
(pages 54–55)

*Continued on //
page 54*

*Continued from
page 52*

To make the red base, combine all the ingredients in a food processor and blend until smooth. Chill for an hour before serving. Repeat the process for the green base.

Set up a self-serve station that includes a carafe each of the red and green base, assortments of vodka and other spirits of your liking, and desired fixin's and garnishes.

Have the guests build their own drinks to their preferred strength and outlandishness by combining the base with the vodka and adding some ice and the garnishes.

## Garnishes and Fixin's for Your Bloody Bar

- Maldon salt
- Celery salt
- Cracked pepper
- Lemon wedges
- Lime wedges
- Worcestershire sauce
- Various hot sauces (of increasing heat)
- Clam juice
- Celery stalks
- Cornichons
- Dill pickle spears
- Pickled asparagus
- Pickled okra
- Olives
- Capers
- Pepperoncini
- Lox
- Cubed cheeses
- Sliders
- Fried chicken fingers
- Peeled shrimp
- Beluga caviar
- Gold flakes

# Making a Flavored Salt Rim

Flavored salt rims are an easy way to fancy up a Bloody Bar if your garnish options are otherwise limited. Start with ½ cup of flaky salt, like Maldon or something fancy a friend brought back from France, and combine it with 2 or 3 teaspoons of a dry flavoring agent of your choice: grated lime or orange zest, crushed red pepper flakes, smoked paprika, dried rosemary, etc.

If you want to use a liquid flavoring agent, like Sriracha, combine it with the salt and dry it in the oven or a microwave.

Spread a shallow layer of the flavored salt on a plate and add it to the self-serve Bloody Bar. Before building a drink, guests should moisten the rim of their glass (rubbing a lime wedge across the top works well) and dip it in the salt, lightly twisting until a thick layer sticks to the rim.

# The Sober Spritzer

Admittedly, some people are able to keep their New Year's resolutions a little longer than till lunchtime. So, mock it or not, many will be attempting Dry January and not drinking for the entire month. If they happen to be a guest in your home, don't tempt them toward failure by only offering them some seltzer. Instead, make 'em a mocktail that is just as tasty as the spiked stuff.

1 cup granulated sugar

10 slices peeled ginger

3 teaspoons juniper berries

1 bay leaf

1 cup fresh grapefruit juice

3 ounces fresh lime juice

Soda water

Grapefruit twists,
for garnish

In a saucepan, combine the sugar, ginger, juniper berries, bay leaf, and grapefruit juice with 2 cups of water and stir. Bring to a boil over high heat, then reduce the heat and let simmer for an hour. Remove from the stove and pour through a fine-mesh strainer. Add the lime juice and stir. Chill before serving.

To make individual drinks, pour 2 to 3 ounces of the concentrate into a highball glass filled with ice and top with soda water, then garnish with a grapefruit twist.

# Hot or Not?

Everyone likes Groundhog Day even if most people can't remember when it actually is until they see some old dude pulling Puxsutawney Phil out of a hole live on CNN. (It's February 2, for the record.) With February lacking many opportunities to party, a Groundhog Day drinking event, right after everyone has finished work for the day, fills the bill nicely. Of course, we'll need a happy hour cocktail that suits whatever the groundhog predicted that morning.

As a popular cocktail instructor in the Detroit area, Tammy Coxen cleverly came up with a dual cocktail named Go, Groundhog, Go! that can be served both hot or cold. When the groundhog sees his shadow, make this drink as a gin-based hot toddy variant, because you're in for six more weeks of winter. If the groundhog doesn't see his shadow, turn this recipe into a light and refreshing drink, perfect for the impending spring.

3 cups gin

1½ cups Cinnamon Syrup (page 17)

6 ounces fresh lemon juice

12 dashes Angostura bitters

48 ounces (6 cups) hot water or 32 ounces soda water (depending on the version you're making)

In a pitcher, pre-batch by combining the gin, syrup, lemon juice, and Angostura bitters.

To make the hot version of the drink, pour 3½ ounces of the batch into a mug and top with 3 ounces of hot water.

To make the cold version of the drink, combine 3½ ounces of the batch in a shaker with ice. Shake well, then strain into a rocks glass filled with ice. Top with 2 ounces of soda water.

# The Big Game Kegged Cocktail

Super Bowl parties are well-known for their gluttony—though most of that pertains to the snacks. Hosts spend all day pulling pork while guests arrive with a potluck of layered dips and baked goods. All the while everyone neglects the drinking aspect. Oh people drink heavily—*do they*—but most folks usually opt for pseudo-American "lite" beers and basic mixed drinks (rum and Coke, gin and tonic, etc.) This year, why not get a keg?

Kegged cocktails have started gaining prominence in the last several years but you could argue they still haven't reached any sort of ubiquity. Certainly not for home usage, although they work great for a party. It'll be a bit of an initial investment to secure the necessary equipment, but it will really up your party game for the rest of time.

Here's a great kegged cocktail recipe created by Tony Gonzalez of Treaty Oak Distilling in Austin. If you prepare it for the Super Bowl, you'll make the batch on Sunday morning and it will serve all your guests all night long. If using a 5-gallon keg (see opposite), it essentially means you'll be making one 640-ounce cocktail!

8 (26-ounce) bottles bourbon

4 cups fresh lime juice

8 cups fresh lemon juice

1 gallon Winter Syrup
(page 23)

½ gallon very cold water

Build the drink by combining all the ingredients in a 5-gallon container before adding to the keg. The water is for dilution since you will not be shaking this drink with ice.

Have the gusts pour their own drinks into red Solo cups directly from the keg.

# But Where to Acquire an Empty Keg?

Believe me, there are far more used kegs out there than you think—though they won't be much cheaper than the new ones you can find on Amazon. Look for ball-lock Cornelius kegs ("Corny" kegs in homebrewer guy parlance) with the large open tops you can dump your cocktail into. Five gallons is the most common size, but you can find 2½-and 3-gallon sizes too (adjust the recipe accordingly). You should be able to find all of the following for $200 to $300.

- **Tap tower with hose**—Your way to dispense from the keg. You could likewise use a picnic tap, similar to what you used to rent for beer kegs in college.

- **$CO_2$ tank**—Five pounds is plenty, which should be enough to get you through two full kegs.

- **Regulator**—For gauging pressure.

- **Air hose**—For connecting the $CO_2$ tank to the Corny keg.

- **Ball lock valve**—Two connections for connecting/disconnecting to the liquid and gas lines.

- **A way to keep things cold**—For a one-night party, a garbage can full of ice works swell.

# I'm with Cupid

People don't really throw Valentine's Day parties. If you're dating someone you usually take that person out to dinner. If you're married to someone you sit at home and talk about how it's Valentine's Day and you should probably do something romantic before you just order some delivery burritos (uh, guilty). If you're single, well, you may go drink yourself silly with your boys or gal pals, or self-loathe at home. Instead, why not invite over all the local area singles you know for some cocktails and possible matchmaking.

One of the first "girly" cocktails to have emerged during the flapper era, the Pink Lady is actually anything but. Though it comes out a beautiful pink color, this is no frilly-tini; it's actually a strong drink with a hefty dose of gin, applejack, and grenadine. This cocktail tweaks the Pink Lady by swapping in pink gin and rose water.

If you're feeling fancy, use your favorite bitters and a spray bottle to stencil symbols or V-day phrases on top of the drinks (or have your guests decorate their own).

6 ounces Gordon's Pink Gin

2 ounce applejack

2 ounce Bitter Truth Rose Water

2 ounce fresh lemon juice

1 ounce Grenadine (page 19)

4 egg whites

Bitters, for garnish (optional)

Combine all the ingredients in a shaker (without ice) and do a dry shake. Add ice and shake hard.

Strain into coupes, and garnish with bitters.

# Spring Cocktails

**S**pring is a time of rebirth, as the sweaters and parkas slowly move to the closet, and drinking outdoors again becomes a possibility. Alas, it's not quite time for the flip-flops and frozen drinks just yet. Thus, these holiday drinks still toe the line between rich and refreshing.

Here you'll find a Mardi Gras cocktail meant to resemble the (in)famous King Cake and an Easter drink served inside a chocolate bunny. There will be a flowery cocktail for Mother's Day and a tree-hugging libation for Arbor Day. Spring is also event season, which will introduce a cinema-inspired sipper for your annual Oscars Party and a Doublemint Julep for the Derby.

# S'morge Washington

Believe it or not, there are only 10 federal holidays in the U.S. of A. (I know, I know, we should move to Scandinavia which has like 50 days off, or so we're told.) Some of these holidays are obvious and you are most certainly going to be drinking heavily on them—Fourth of July, Christmas, Thanksgiving, New Year's Day, and the like. Others you may treat as just another day of no-work/more-drink, but it wouldn't be all that reverential to have a party for the occasion (think MLK Day).

Then there's George Washington's Birthday (aka Presidents' Day). George Washington brewed beer, sold whiskey—and, like most other presidents—was a drinker. Plus, you have Monday off work, so why not have some friends over and serve them a S'morge Washington? A safer version of our first president's favorite drink—a mixture of beer, rum, and molasses warmed up and caramelized with a flaming red fireplace poker—this cocktail leans more toward every child's favorite campfire treat.

3 ounces High West
Campfire whiskey

4½ ounces Marshmallow
Syrup (page 19)

3 eggs

2 (12-ounce) bottles bock
beer

Marshmallows, for garnish

In a heat-resistant pitcher, stir together the whiskey, syrup, and eggs. Meanwhile, in a saucepan, heat the beer over medium heat for a few minutes until it is steaming, but not boiling. Very slowly (so the eggs do not scramble) pour the hot beer into the whiskey mixture while whisking. Pour the mixture back and forth between two pitchers several times until frothy.

Divide among mugs. Spear a few marshmallows on toothpicks and toast by flaming with a culinary torch, then use to garnish.

# Our Presidents' Favorite Cocktails

Or, you could just serve every guest *their* favorite president's favorite drink at this party. A few notables.

- **John Adams**—An entire "tankard" of cider, preferably in the morning.

- **Ulysses S. Grant**—Old Crow whiskey, especially while taking down the Confederacy.

- **William McKinley**—His eponymous cocktail, McKinley's Delight, comprised of rye, sweet vermouth, cherry brandy, and absinthe.

- **Teddy Roosevelt**—Mint Juleps, preferably using mint from the White House garden.

- **Herbert Hoover**—A double martini, which he liked so much he even pounded one on his deathbed.

- **FDR**—Pretty much anything, but especially the Rum Swizzle, a sailor's sipper made with Bermuda rum and lime juice.

- **Harry Truman**—Old-fashioneds.

- **JFK**—Bloody Marys, and lots of 'em.

- **LBJ**—Copious scotch and sodas, prepared by Secret Service men.

- **Gerald Ford**—Martinis, preferably three of them with lunch.

- **Ronald Reagan**—The Orange Blossom Special, a childish combo of vodka, grenadine, and orange juice.

# The Box Office

In America, many of our top occasions for throwing parties revolve around the TV. Yes, between Super Bowls and Kentucky Derbies, that usually means sports. But, for non-sportsball revelers, the Academy Awards offer a model occasion to have folks over to snark on dresses, guess the winners ("Really?!"), and booze it up on a Sunday night.

Created by Peter Szigeti, general manager of The Ghost Walks, this drink was inspired by the bar's location within Boston's Theater District, and befits the occasion. Savory, buttery, and just a little boozy, it's great for washing down handfuls of salty popcorn. And the way Szigeti proposes you serve it solves the eternal struggle of how to hold *both* your drink and snacks while at a party—you'll need plastic to-go cups with lids and popcorn boxes for this clever creation.

5 cups bourbon

2½ cups PX sherry

2½ cups butterscotch syrup

3½ cups blood orange puree

2½ cups fresh lemon juice

Popcorn, for serving (optional)

In a pitcher, pre-batch by combining the bourbon, sherry, butterscotch syrup, and blood orange puree and refrigerate until ready to use.

To make individual drinks, combine 3 ounces of the batch with ½ ounce lemon juice and ice in a cocktail shaker. Shake and then pour everything (including the ice) into a plastic cup, cover with a lid, and insert a long straw. Place the cup in the bottom of a popcorn box or bucket, then load the space around and above the drink with popcorn so only the straw is peeking out.

# Every-Four-Years Cocktail

Sometimes our culture can't simply enjoy the present but can only think about the future. That's why pumpkin beers hit the shelves in August and Christmas decorations go up the day after Halloween. Then there's a holiday that always seems to be in the future—it only comes once every four years.

Increasingly, people are using the odd elusiveness of Leap Day to throw parties; if you get one "extra" day this year, you might as well use it to have fun. That's why Brooklyn bartender Andrew White created a Leap Day libation. The inclusion of rhubarb is an obscure callback to an episode of *30 Rock* in which the characters celebrate their own Leap Day traditions.

6 ounces vodka

2 ounces Aperol

4 ounces Rhubarb Syrup (page 21)

12 dashes Regan's Orange Bitters

8 to 12 ounces soda water

Rhubarb stalks, for garnish

Strawberry wedges, for garnish

In a pitcher, pre-batch by combining the vodka, Aperol, syrup, and bitters.

To make individual drinks, pour 3 ounces of the batch into a highball glass filled with ice, then top with 2 to 3 ounces of soda water. Garnish with a rhubarb stalk and a strawberry wedge.

# King Cake Old Fashioned

While everyone else is partying in the streets, taking their shirts off, and slamming Hurricanes, why not have a more refined Mardi Gras party at your home? King Cake is the iconic dish of the carnival season, and hundreds of thousands of these circular purple-, green-, and yellow-sugared brioche cakes are consumed in New Orleans each February and March.

Local restaurant SoBou makes special Mardi Gras–inspired cocktails every year and this King Cake analog may be their most evocative—and quite easy to adapt for your own at-home party.

1 cup Plantation Stiggins' Fancy Pineapple Rum

1 cup overproof Jamaican rum

2 ounces Cinnamon Syrup (page 17)

2 ounces Toasted Pecan and Brown Sugar Syrup (page 22)

Splash of pure vanilla extract

4 dashes El Guapo Holiday Pie Bitters

King cake baby ice cubes (page 73)

Lemon peels, for garnish

In a pitcher, pre-batch by combining both rums, both syrups, vanilla extract, and the bitters.

To make individual drinks, pour 2½ ounces of the batch into a rocks glass filled with ice (use at least one king cake baby ice cube), and stir. Garnish with a lemon peel.

# King Cake
# Baby Ice

Traditionally, a small plastic baby is hidden in each King cake—whoever is lucky enough to stumble upon the baby is said to be granted prosperity for the year. SoBou continues that tradition in their cocktail, though you'd have to be pretty blotto not to notice a baby in your ice!

To pull the stunt off, order some small plastic or metallic King cake babies from a mom 'n' pop producer (or on Amazon, if you must). Plant the babies in an ice tray and then pour water on top of them. Freeze and voila! Babies in ice. Parker encourages doing the same for tiny crowns, necklaces, and anything Mardi Gras related, noting: "Just make sure your guests know they're there!"

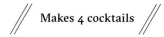
# The Chocolate Bunny-ful of Bourbon

You've gathered with your family on a lovely Sunday in spring, you've got your best pastels on, you're snacking on Peeps, and the beautiful ham is about to arrive on the brunch table. If only you had an appropriate drink. Unfortunately, there's never really been an apt Easter cocktail.

Luckily, Jamie Boudreau of Seattle's Canon: Whiskey and Bitters Emporium bucks the trend with his cocktail Esther Bunny IV, Esq. You can easily make them for the adults while the kids are searching for the eggs you never hid.

4 ounces bourbon

2 ounces Punt e Mes

1 ounce Fernet-Branca

1 ounce Crème de Menthe

1 ounce Triple Sec

12 dashes Angostura bitters

4 hollow milk chocolate bunnies (optional for serving)

In a mixing glass filled with ice, combine all the ingredients and stir together to mix. Carefully strain into rocks glasses.

To serve in a chocolate bunny, unwrap the bunny and carefully make a small hole in the ear. Using a small funnel, pour the drink into the bunny and gently push a straw through the open ear hole to serve. (Boudreau suggests placing the bunny in a rocks glass before inserting the straw just in case you squeeze too hard and break it.)

*Pictured on page 62*

## Cadbury Creme Egg Shots

You could also make these Easter-themed candy shots. Remove the foil from Cadbury Creme Eggs and carefully slice them in half with a serrated knife. Scoop out the filling and mix in a bowl with ½ ounce Bourbon Cream and 1 ounce bourbon per egg. Carefully fill the Creme Egg cavities, and shoot!

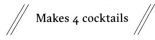
# The Seder Slake

A lot of people will repeat the stereotype that Jews don't drink, but drinking is an integral part of quite a few of our holidays. Passover is a biggie on the calendar, not "fun" per se, but still a time we gather around the dinner table to commemorate the story of the Israelites' exodus from Egypt upon being freed from slavery. In turn, we are "obligated" (it literally says so in the Torah!) to drink four glasses of wine throughout the night.

But what if your guests don't think a glass of Kosher wine looks cool on Insta? There's no reason you can't serve a Passover-friendly cocktail . . . or four.

This New York Sour variant includes all Kosher-for-Passover ingredients (meaning a non-grain spirit such as tequila as the base), while evoking the Seder plate with the egg white and charoseth syrup, and, yes, even a Manischewitz wine floater if you want to be at least *somewhat* pious.

1 cup reposado tequila

3 ounces Charoseth Syrup (page 17)

2 ounces fresh lemon juice

2 ounces fresh lime juice

4 egg whites

2 ounces Manischewitz wine

Combine the tequila, syrup, lemon and lime juice, and the egg whites in a shaker (without ice) and do a dry shake. Add ice and shake hard.

Strain into wine glasses and top each with ½ ounce of the wine.

# The Inoffensive Tipperary

While St. Patrick's Day is in many ways *the* party holiday, many non–Irish Americans now use it as a canvas for some of their most culturally offensive partying tendencies. We've made it less a day of Irish pride, and more one of dressing like a fool ("Irish I Was Drunker" T-shirts), drinking green beer and (eek) "car bombs," and throwing up in the street.

Be better than that, and when you have your buddies over on March 17, serve them something classy that an Irish person would actually drink. Since the early twentieth century, this has probably become the most famous Irish cocktail (that doesn't involve coffee). Somewhat of a Manhattan variant, the original recipe called for equal parts of every ingredient—modern bartenders typically opt to lighten up on the sweeter elements as in this recipe.

1 cup Irish whiskey

4 ounces sweet vermouth

2 ounces green chartreuse
(or use as a rinse on
each glass)

In a mixing glass filled with ice, combine all the ingredients and stir together.
　　Strain into individual coupes.

# Hamantaschen Mojito

Purim might be the *only* holiday all year—anywhere on the planet—where getting drunk is baked into the actual religious observance. Even for the children. That makes it ideal for hosting an all-ages celebration.

Kind of like Halloween for Jews, kids are supposed to dress in costumes, while everyone drinks heavily and yells at the atrocities once committed against us in ancient Persia. But just because we're supposed to get drunk on Purim doesn't mean we should pound Bud Heavys and throw back Fireball shots.

This recipe comes from Ohio-based, Kosher-keeping recipe designer Alison Gütwaks, who decided to take a stab at making cocktail-flavored hamantaschen. Traditionally this Purim pastry is filled with, uh, not-exactly-popular flavors like prune and poppyseed, but Gütwaks started producing ones with fillings reminiscent of cocktails. All of them include alcohol, though it mostly bakes off so kids can enjoy them, while the adults indulge in the actual drinks they are based on.

2 teaspoons granulated sugar

2 mint sprigs

1 lime, quartered

2 ounces white rum

Soda water

Mojito Hamantaschen, for serving (recipe opposite)

In a highball glass, combine the sugar and mint leaves then lightly muddle to release their oils. Add the lime quarters and muddle to release their juices. Add ice and the rum and stir.

Top with the soda water and serve with a Mojito Hamantaschen.

*Pictured on pages 62–63*

# Mojito Hamantaschen

Makes about 30 pastries

## FOR THE DOUGH:

2 cups all-purpose flour, plus more for dusting

¾ teaspoon baking powder

⅛ teaspoon kosher salt

1 stick unsalted butter, softened

⅔ cup granulated sugar

1 large egg

1 egg yolk, egg white reserved

1 teaspoon pure vanilla extract

1 teaspoon peppermint oil

1 tablespoon minced fresh mint leaves

## FOR THE LIME-RUM CURD FILLING:

1 cup granulated sugar

1 stick unsalted butter

¼ cup cornstarch

6 ounces fresh lime juice

1 tablespoon lime zest

2 tablespoons rum

2 large eggs

Demerara sugar, for sprinkling

To make the dough, combine the flour, baking powder, and salt in a bowl, and set aside.

In another bowl, beat the butter until creamy, then stir in the sugar and mix until fluffy. Next, stir in the egg, egg yolk, vanilla, peppermint oil, and mint leaves. Finally, add the flour mixture to the egg mixture and mix until a crumbly dough forms. Using your hands, knead the dough until smooth. Divide the dough in half, wrap each half in plastic wrap, and refrigerate overnight. Cover the reserved egg white and refrigerate.

To make the filling, combine the sugar, butter, cornstarch, lime juice, lime zest, and rum in a saucepan and cook over medium heat until the butter melts. Meanwhile, beat the eggs in a bowl. Slowly pour the eggs into the saucepan (so they don't scramble), whisking constantly until the mixture starts to boil and thicken. Whisk for about 1 minute, then remove from heat. Refrigerate the curd until ready to use.

Preheat the oven to 375°F. Line two large cookie sheets with parchment paper. Roll out the refrigerated dough on a lightly floured surface until it is about ⅛-inch thick. Cut out rounds using a cookie cutter and place a dollop of the curd in the center of each round. Dip your pinky in the reserved egg white and lightly wet the edges of each piece. Make the hamantaschen triangle shape by folding the bottom to make two corners and folding the top to make the third. Brush the outer part of the hamantaschen with the egg white and sprinkle with the demerara sugar. Bake for about 12 minutes until lightly browned. Serve on a platter alongside Hamantaschen Mojitos.

# Doublemint Juleps

Another indispensable invite-people-over-to-drink-in-front-of-the-TV event, the Kentucky Derby is, quite frankly, better than the Super Bowl or Academy Awards. Why? Because you have to pay attention to the screen for only two minutes. The rest of the time can be spent either preparing drinks . . . or drinking them.

The Derby is also great because, again, unlike the big game or Oscars, it has its own signature cocktail—one that most folks don't drink on any other day of the year. That, of course, is the Mint Julep and, since it is somewhat labor intensive to crank out all afternoon, why not just make a big batch of these Doublemint Juleps instead?

18 ounces high-proof bourbon (Blanton's Bourbon is a great choice and has a horse stopper–capped bottle which can be used for serving)

6 ounces Mint Syrup (page 20)

Soda water (optional)

Mint sprigs, for garnish

In a pitcher, combine the bourbon with the syrup, then pour into the original Blanton's bottle.

Have the guests make their own drinks by packing their cups with crushed ice and pouring 2 to 2½ ounces of the mixture over it. (If you don't have crushed ice capabilities in your freezer, put standard ice in a canvas bag and smash repeatedly with a mallet.) Guests can top with soda water for a lighter drink, and garnish with the mint sprigs.

## The Sonic Ice Trick

For the Mint Julep you would ideally use that soft, chewable "pebble" or "pellet" ice—but unless you have some $5,000 machine like they use at high-end bars, you probably can't make any at home. But what if you live near a Sonic Drive-In? They use the same kind of ice in their delicious sodas and limeades. And they will let you buy it for $2 per bag—per *10 pound* bag—so make room in the freezer.

# Quiet Company

No holiday has become more of a contrarian excuse to party than Arbor Day. Seriously. Perhaps this simple holiday that encourages the planting of trees also encourages the act of playful lampooning. Or maybe in today's increasingly busy busy busy world the thought of a relaxing respite among nature really seems like something worth celebrating.

"I've always thought of trees as being my quiet company while camping alone," claims Tyler Stevens of PDX's Pink Rabbit. His uniquely nature-like drink is thus perfect for a little Arbor Day tree-planting party. Have some buddies over to help dig holes and place roots—a few cocktails will make it all the more fun. Or indulge in some solo drinking in the woods, if you must.

1 cup Mezcal Union

1 cup Lindemans Pêche

1 cup Fever-Tree Indian Tonic Water

Fresh local herbs like rosemary, thyme, or lavender, for garnish

Lemon wedges, for garnish

In a pitcher, pre-batch by combining the mezcal, pêche, and tonic water, and refrigerate until ready to use.

To make individual drinks, pour 6 ounces of the batch into a highball glass and top with ice. Garnish with the fresh herbs and a lemon wedge.

# Bantha Milk

As we all sink deeper and deeper into an artificial online world, it only makes sense that we would soon start celebrating made-up holidays too. Then again, all holidays were "made up" at one time. May the Fourth, or Star Wars Day, emerged in 2011 when someone realized that "May the Fourth" kinda sounds like "may the force" and, oh boy, that's enough for something to go viral in this day and age.

The Cottonmouth Club, one of the top cocktail bars in Houston, decided to commemorate the holiday with an entire menu of Star Wars–themed drinks, like Hoth Park Swizzle, Java the Hutt, and this blue cocktail better known to die-hard fans as Bantha Milk. In the movie, this boozy wake-up drink was quaffed by Aunt Beru, unbeknownst to her whiny teen nephew and buzzkill husband.

1¾ ounces gin

½ ounce blue curaçao

¾ ounce fresh lemon juice

½ ounce Classic Simple Syrup (page 16)

3 drops rose water

1 egg white

Soda water

Combine the gin, curaçao, lemon juice, syrup, rose water, and egg white in a shaker (without ice) and do a dry shake. Add ice and shake hard.

Strain into a highball glass without ice. Top with the soda water, pouring as much as you can down the side of the glass. The carbonation should cause the frothy head to rise above the top of the glass.

# The Inoffensive Paloma

Yet another non-American occasion that is so often celebrated offensively by Americans who have given it the unfortunate "Cinco de Drinko" moniker. It's sadly become less about commemorating Mexico's victory over the French Empire and more about gringos dressing like fools (fake mustaches, "comically" large sombreros) and drinking cheap buckets of Corona and pitchers of margarita.

Believe it or not, most citizens of Mexico are not going to be drinking giant goblets of margaritas, but are more likely to opt for this simpler mixed drink which works great as a late-spring cooler.

2 ounces tequila

6 ounces grapefruit soda (look for Squirt or Jarritos)

Lime wedges, plus extra slices, for garnish

Pour the tequila into a highball glass filled with ice. Top with the grapefruit soda, and squeeze a few lime wedges over the top, then garnish with lime slices.

# A Drinkable Arrangement

Mother's Day is a holiday you absolutely have to celebrate with at least one person—mom. This is usually done at brunch at a nice restaurant where mom is fed and fêted and gifted and glorified and her kids even urge her to kick back with a mimosa or two.

But if you really want to show mom you care, why not try hosting her at a homemade brunch in her honor, where you serve this large format cocktail which relies heavily on floral components like yellow chartreuse and the Carthusian monk liqueur infused with carnations (the ultimate Mother's Day flower). Mom can opt to split her "gift" with the family, or go solo if she's in the mood for a boozy afternoon.

1 cup gin

4 ounces Yellow Chartreuse

4 ounces St-Germain

6 ounces fresh lime juice

4 ounces honey

1 (750-milliliter) bottle rosé

In a vase that can be poured, pre-batch by combining the gin, Yellow Chartreuse, St-Germain, lime juice, and honey, along with a large handful of ice. Stir well until chilled and a bit frothy.

To build a drink, pour 2 to 3 ounces into a highball glass filled with ice and top with the rosé.

## Mail Mom a Cocktail

If you're a bad son or daughter who moved far, far away from mom, consider preparing the above cocktail in a bottle that can be sealed airtight (adding 5 ounces of water instead of ice) and overnighting it—as well as a bottle of rosé—to mom. Include a card that tells her how to prepare the cocktail and how much you love her.

# Summer Cocktails

**T**o some, summer itself is one long, three-month holiday. Perhaps that's why there are fewer "official" occasions to get festive, and probably why so many people pick the summer as the time to celebrate their life's most important occasions—weddings, reunions, gender reveals, and the like.

Drinks for this season will be light in ABV, full of ice, and meant to keep you on your feet from sunup to sundown. These will be produce-heavy cocktails as well—like a Memorial Day treat full of beets and an Independence Day punch made with watermelon juice.

Summer cocktails are also a little silly—Father's Day will offer a chance to serve a total "dad" drink, while the gender reveal party cocktail will truly stun your guests.

# The Apartment Farmer

Summer kicks off with another one of those holidays that no one really knows what it's about, everyone just knows they get an extra weekend day to drink. No matter where you live, it should be getting warm by now and, perhaps, Memorial Day is your first chance to have friends over to drink in your backyard. Why not honor that with a uniquely outdoorsy cocktail?

Jay Sanders of Kansas City's Manifesto and SoT designed this cocktail to specifically not look like a drink. Instead, it appears to be a recently potted plant. But now that summer is here, it's time to drink this plant, burst through the soil of spring, and come to life! You could have a whole bunch of these cocktails lined up for guests as they arrive. They wouldn't even know it's a drink until you plunge a straw through the "soil" and serve it to them.

6 ounces blanco tequila

½ cup Fresh Beet Juice (page 94)

3 ounces Giffard Crème de Mûre Blackberry Liqueur

2 ounces sherry (use Alvear Cream or Amontillado)

3 ounces fresh lime juice

4 egg whites

Edible Dirt Dust, for garnish (page 94)

Baby beets or radishes, for garnish

In a shaker with ice, combine the tequila, beet juice, blackberry liqueur, sherry, lime juice, and egg whites and shake. Strain out the ice and shake again.

Divide the mixture among four plant pots (see note on page 94). Allow the liquid to sit long enough so the egg white separates and forms a froth on top. Cover with some edible dirt dust and tuck in a baby beet or radish.

# Fresh Beet Juice

Makes 1 cup

½ cup raw beets, peeled
and chopped

½ cup hot water

Fill a blender with the beets and add the hot water. Puree until smooth. Use a cheesecloth to strain out the solids.


# Edible Dirt Dust

Makes 1½ cups

½ cup cocoa powder

½ cup ground cinnamon

½ cup dehydrated cascara
(coffee fruit)

In a spice grinder, combine all the ingredients and grind until you achieve a dirt-like consistency.


# Getting Your Own Flower Pot Mugs

Admittedly, the most nettlesome yet critical part of this entire cocktail is the serving vessel. You can't just pour your drink into a real flowerpot. Not only is the clay or whatever it's made of probably not safe to drink from, there's the bigger issue of the small drainage holes at the bottom. A cocktail blooper just waiting to happen!

Lining a pot with a ziplock bag or plastic wrap before building the drink is a workaround, though an inelegant one. Sanders actually uses custom-made mugs that look just like flowerpots, but there are plenty of other drink-safe options online for you to use.

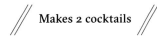

# Daddy Drunkest

Dads are, perhaps deservingly, less celebrated than moms. There's never really a big to-do for Father's Day, and dad is lucky if his children let him watch some exhilarating PGA golf for a few hours on CBS before presenting him with a bottle of midlevel scotch they read about in *Esquire* just yesterday.

But it doesn't have to be that way. Like with mom, who deserves all the flowers and hugs and dainty pink cocktails you can possibly afford, you can have a little more fun with pops. And, I'm not just saying all this because *I am a dad.*

This cocktail is a perfectly thoughtful gift for the family patriarch who'd rather spend the day relaxing on the couch with his entire family around him than at some schmancy, crowded restaurant.

2 (12-ounce) cans Budweiser, chilled

3 ounces dad's favorite scotch

2 ounces fresh lemon juice

1 ounce Ginger Syrup (page 18)

Dump or drink about 3 ounces of each beer can. Divide the scotch, lemon juice, and syrup equally among the cans and give them a gentle stir.

If dad's up for it, place the cans in a beer guzzler helmet (à la Homer Simpson) and attach the straws, so dad can enjoy his drinks without lifting a finger all day.

# Watermelon Punch

Independence Day is a day of goofing off, perfect for inviting buddies over to slug G&Ts on your deck or pound brewskis on your roof. It's a day of freedom, 'murica, and time off work. We celebrate by eating gut-busting cased meats our doctors have advised us against, and by drinking ourselves silly among good company.

And, so often, we try to show our patriotism by slugging quality products from the good ol' U.S. of A. Like this punch designed by Dan Oskey, co-founder of Minneapolis's Tattersall Distilling, which offers a presentation your guests won't soon forget. It also allows you to prep drinks on July 3, well before you put on that Old Glory tank top and start lighting firecrackers.

1 watermelon, flesh scooped out (keep shell for serving if desired)

2 cups gin

1 cup dry vermouth

1 cup fresh lime juice

4 ounces maple syrup

Remove all the seeds from the watermelon flesh and place it in a blender. Blend on high until smooth; this should yield about 4 cups of juice.

In a punch bowl combine the watermelon juice, gin, vermouth, lime juice, and syrup and stir. Chill until ready to serve.

Serve in a punch bowl with a ladle or in the watermelon shell tapped with a spigot (see page 117).

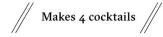

# Frozen Cake Shake

You get gifts, well-wishes, steak dinners, Facebook messages, candles and cake, and sometimes even a special song from the waiters when it's your birthday. But it doesn't seem like anyone ever gets a special birthday cocktail. Up the ante this year for the age-changing people in your life with this frozen shake.

Michael Boughton, the beverage director at The Smoke Shop in Boston, wanted to create a drink that mimics the ice cream cakes he likes to be served on his own birthday. He didn't just want to re-create a liquidized form of the cake . . . he wanted a boozy version of literally the best bite. "The best part of ice cream cake is that spoonful of semi-melted vanilla ice cream with a healthy dose of chocolate cookie crumble," Boughton explains. "That spoonful is what I was looking to re-create with this cocktail."

4 ounces white rum

2 ounces Drillaud White Cocoa Crème de Cacao

1 ounce Classic Simple Syrup (page 16)

2 pints premium vanilla ice cream, softened at room temperature

Oreo cookie crumbles, for garnish

In a blender, combine the rum, Crème de Cacao, syrup, vanilla extract, and ice cream and blend on high until smooth.

Pour into cocktail glasses with straws. Garnish with the cookie crumbles, and a lit candle for the birthday boy or girl.

# Pimm's and Hers Cup

Weddings are the ultimate party and while midlevel Champagne alongside a single red and white option used to be enough for the open bar, today's brides and grooms are going bigger. Often, that means having a special "couple's cocktail." Of course, these can't be too expensive to put together, too tricky for the cater waiters to whip up, nor so boozy that grandma is wobbly before the first dance. Mostly, this means taking a cocktail that already exists and giving it a matrimonious name, heavy on the puns.

For my wedding we served this Pimm's Cup variant made with seasonal, local fruits. With a mid-August wedding in New England, that meant a heavy dose of berries and cherries. No matter what fruits you opt for, this light and refreshing cocktail is perfect for kicking off a late-afternoon cocktail hour—the English liqueur's supposedly digestive properties are a great way to soothe the stomach before a few hours of eating, drinking, and dancing.

2 cups mix of local fruits, plus more for garnish (see page 102)

2 cups Pimm's No. 1 Cup

4 ounces fresh lemon juice

2 ounces Classic Simple Syrup (page 16)

4 cups lemonade or lemon soda

In a pitcher, muddle the fruits. Add ice along with the remaining ingredients and stir together.

Pour into highball glasses, making sure each serving gets some fruit and ice. Garnish with more fruit and serve.

# Ideas for Local Fruit and Booze Combos

- **Northeast**—Opt for a variety of chopped apples and pears. Adding some apple brandy and topping with a fizzy cider as opposed to lemon soda might be nice as well. This flavor profile works particularly well for an autumnal wedding, especially if garnished with cinnamon sticks.

- **Midwest**—Smashed cherries and strawberries would work great. For the sweetener, use a local honey or even a particularly sweet mead.

- **The South**—Use oranges, peaches, and even mangoes. You can additionally swap in sweet tea instead of lemonade—or better yet, use both, making an "Arnold Palmer" Pimm's Cup. Perfect for an outdoor wedding on a hot day.

- **Southwest**—How 'bout a Pimm's with a bit of a kick? Chopped chilis can add some nice heat. Heat that you might want to cool down with some agave instead of a mere simple syrup.

- **Pacific Northwest**—Crush some grapes or use frozen ones as your ice cubes. Top with sparkling wine instead of lemonade.

# Cold Buttered Rum

If some people spend all winter thinking about warm weather, there are others who spend all summer wishing it was winter. Increasingly, people are starting to throw cheeky "Christmas in July" parties. Nothing's more fun than having your friends come over in shorts, flip-flops, and Santa hats—and then gorging on the kinds of 1,000-calorie creamy libations that define the holiday season (and will ruin their hard-earned bikini bodies).

Luckily, there is a minor canon of "wintery" drinks paradoxically perfect for a hotter-than-hell July day. Todd Thrasher, a DC-area bartender and owner of Tiki TNT, has long offered a Cold Buttered Rum which is a fun take on the emerging holiday. Blast The Beach Boys' *Christmas Album* and whip some up.

2 ounces Buttered Rum Mix (page 104)

1½ ounces Spice Mixture (page 104)

Orange twist, for garnish

In a mixing glass, combine the buttered rum mix and the spice mixture with ice and stir gently for 1 minute.

Strain into a rocks glass over a large piece of ice. Garnish with an orange twist.

# Buttered Rum Mix

Makes 1 liter

½ pound unsalted butter

1 liter spiced rum

In a small saucepan, melt the butter over low heat until it starts foaming, about 3 minutes. Remove from heat and skim off the foam, then let sit for 5 minutes. A solid white residue will settle to the bottom of the pan. Carefully pour the buttered rum into a container, making sure to leave the residue behind in the pan. Wipe out the pan and pour the butter back in. Heat over low heat, making sure the butter remains liquid and no solids start to form, for about 2 minutes. Remove from heat and add the spiced rum. Stir until combined. Transfer the mixture to a plastic container and chill in the freezer overnight.

When you take the container out in the morning, the butterfat will have risen to the top above the rum, which will not freeze. Skim the frozen butterfat off and discard, then strain the rest through a fine mesh strainer until solids are completely eliminated. Bottle and refrigerate until ready to use or up to 2 weeks.

# Spice Mixture

Makes 24 ounces

2 cups light brown sugar

5 cloves

5 allspice berries

5 cardamom pods

1½ star anise

1 cinnamon stick

¼ ounce grated nutmeg

1 orange peel (no pith)

In a pot, bring 4 cups of water to a boil. Add the sugar and stir until completely dissolved. Reduce to a simmer and add the remaining ingredients. Simmer for 1 hour, letting it reduce by half. Remove from heat and refrigerate overnight. The next morning, strain into a container and refrigerate until ready to use or up to 2 weeks.

# Other Boozy Treats for a Wintery Summer Celebration

Is drinking butter on a hot July day not really your jam? Too bad. The small canon of cocktails for this holiday mostly include butter or something almost as fat-tastic.

- **Christmas in July**—From Brooklyn cocktail bar stalwart The Clover Club, this aptly named drink combines brown butter fat-washed rum with coffee ice cream.

- **The Kris Kringle Colada**—A Manhattan-based Christmas tiki pop-up, Sippin' Santa, offers a variety of drinks that work perfectly for the holiday. None better, however, than this combination of dark Jamaican rum, Cynar, allspice liqueur, lime juice, pineapple juice, and Coco Lopez.

- **You Butter Bet Your Life**—Chicago's South Water Kitchen may have closed in 2017, but their Christmas in the Tropics cocktail, combining Rhum Clement and blackstrap rum along with orange curaçao, mango nectar, and a cardamom-butter syrup, still reigns supreme.

# It's a . . . Cocktail!

In recent years, one of the most popular excuses for getting friends and family together is for what's known as a gender reveal party, where expecting couples divulge the sex of the baby they are expecting. There are so many options to choose from when thinking of the ultimate way to reveal your baby's gender: by slicing open a cake (to see if the inside is blue or pink), by cracking open a piñata to see what gender of toy dolls are inside, or even by unleashing a pink or blue smoke bomb into the sky.

There's a tastier way. A way that won't have your guests brushing pink or blue confetti out of their hair. Serve them a cocktail along with a shot of a blue liquid that, upon pouring in, will either stain the cocktail blue or pink. Gender revealed!

1 ounce vodka

1 ounce fresh lime juice, strained (use a fine mesh strainer until clear)

1 ounce Lemongrass Syrup (page 19)

1½ ounces blue curaçao (if it's a boy)

1½ ounces Butterfly Blue Pea Flower–Infused Gin (if it's a girl), (recipe follows)

In a shaker with ice, combine the vodka, lime juice, and syrup, and shake. Strain into a coupe or cocktail glass.

Give each guest their own cocktail and then a shot glass of either the curaçao or the Butterfly Blue Pea Flower–Infused Gin, depending on the gender.

At the exact same time, have all the guests pour their shots into their cocktails. If it's a boy, the cocktail will turn blue. If it's a girl, the cocktail will turn pink due to the butterfly pea flower coming into contact with the acid of the lime juice.

# Butterfly Blue Pea Flower-Infused Gin

Makes about 24 ounces

10 grams dried butterfly blue pea flowers

1 (750-milliliter) bottle gin

1 teaspoon baking soda (optional)

Remove the green portion of the flowers and place the petals in a large container. Cover with the gin and shake the container. Let sit for a day or two or until it has turned dark blue.

Strain out the petals and pour back into the original gin bottle. You may add more gin if you want to lighten the color. You can also add the baking soda to make the gin more blue.

# Ring of Ice Sipper

All good things must come to an end, and so too does summer. Whether officially the culmination or not, the three-day Labor Day weekend always feels like the end. It feels like the last chance to have friends over for an outdoor, fancy-free party—starting Tuesday it'll be time to buckle down with fall, get back to serious work, have less time for frivolity. Ugh.

This cocktail from Cammie Rae Mitchener of John Brown Underground in Lawrence, Kansas, was designed for making the Labor Day weekend feel just a little longer. It includes both absinthe and LaCroix (not to mention a molded ice ring), but it's easy to make and—at a pretty low proof—even easier to drink as you and your friends fret about the leaves changing color, the days getting shorter, and, oh shoot, there's work tomorrow isn't there?

12 ounces raspberries

1¼ cups Copper & Kings Absinthe Alembic Blanche

1¼ cups John D. Taylor's Velvet Falernum Liqueur

1¼ cups pineapple juice

1¼ cups fresh lime juice

2 (12-ounce) cans LaCroix kiwi sandía

Mint sprigs, for garnish

Freeze half of the raspberries in some water in a large round mold (silicone tube pans work well). Arrange the other half of the raspberries in a single layer on a small tray, then place in the freezer for a few hours.

In a large, chilled punch bowl, combine the absinthe, Falernum, and pineapple and lime juice. Pour in the LaCroix and top with the raspberry ice ring and the individual frozen berries.

Serve in punch glasses and garnish with the mint sprigs.

# Fall
# Cocktails

**F**all is a season of rapid change. So quickly we go from drinking Frosé outdoors to bundling up and needing something a little more cozy. Thus, these holiday drinks will toe the line between refreshing punches and boozy warmers.

There's a cooler served inside an actual Igloo Cooler for tailgating purposes, and a Cranberry Punch for the Thanksgiving feast. There's a frozen Greyhound for après-ski, and a pumpkin-spiced sipper served inside an actual pumpkin. The most thematic gelatin shot comes skull-shaped for Dia de Los Muertos, and the final recipe in this book is the perfect nightcap for when you've had enough of it all.

# The Igloo Cooler . . . Cooler

Every weekend in the fall, millions gather in some of the finest stadium parking lots throughout America for the joyous act of pregaming. Sure, there's going to be a game in, oh, maybe 12 hours, but eating and drinking in the parking lot is honestly the best part.

Unfortunately, just like many party hosts have quit doing anything all too innovative, many tailgaters have also quit doing anything all too out there, instead popping the trunk on their Camry to reveal a cooler of lite beers and some Oscar Meyer weiners.

Tailgating with style need not be difficult. And, just like for a party at home, it's easy to pre-batch a large format drink that people can serve themselves. There'll be some noted differences of course: you're in a parking lot surrounded by asphalt, drunken yokels, and porta-potties, now is not the time to break out the Waterford crystal punch bowl. Instead, opt for something you'll see later in the day on the football sidelines—one of those big, orange, 5-gallon Igloo coolers.

25 cucumbers, peeled and coarsely chopped, plus extra slices for garnish

8 (750-milliliter) bottles gin

12½ cups lime juice (about 60 limes), plus extra wedges for garnish

12½ cups Classic Simple Syrup (page 16)

Soda water or tonic (optional)

Puree the cucumbers in a food processor or a juicer until you get a pulpy juice. Strain through a mesh colander.

In an Igloo cooler, combine the cucumber juice, gin, lime juice, and syrup, and stir. Top the cooler with ice.

Guests can serve themselves directly from the spigot, then top with the soda water for a lighter drink, and garnish with the cucumber slices and lime wedges.

# Punch-kin

Halloween is the one holiday where hosts unfairly put the onus for fun on their guests. Just because people dressed up in costumes doesn't mean you can get away with simply hanging up a few cardboard skeletons you bought from the bargain bin at Walgreens and putting out a bowl of assorted "fun-size" Hershey bars next to a cooler of pumpkin beers.

Instead, why not make a punch your guests will truly remember—and one that will guarantee a great party whether the attendees are the kind of adults that like to cosplay, or whether they're spoilsports who attend the party still in plain clothes. Think pumpkin with a spigot and dry ice (see opposite page).

4 ounces maple syrup

1 (15-ounce) can pumpkin puree

3 (12-ounce) bottles Southern Tier Pumking Imperial Ale

2¼ cups hard cider

1½ cups rye whiskey

1½ cups apple brandy

Ground cinnamon and cinnamon sticks, for garnish

Hollowed out pumpkin, for serving (optional)

In a large punch bowl, combine the syrup and pumpkin puree. Make sure they are well integrated before adding the beer, cider, whiskey, and brandy. Add ice to the punch bowl and stir to chill and dilute the mixture. (If it's too chunky, just add more beer or cider and keep stirring.)

Serve in the punch bowl with a ladle or in the hollowed out pumpkin tapped with a spigot (see opposite). Keep the ground cinnamon and sticks nearby so guests can garnish their drinks.

# The Pumpkin Punch Bowl Hack

Procure the largest pumpkin you can possibly carry home from the store. Remove the stem with a large circular cut. Get someone else to completely gut the pumpkin because that's disgusting. (Choose the first early arriver who asks "Can I help ya with anything?") Make sure the inside is smooth and free of seeds and stringy junk. In theory, you now have a pumpkin punch bowl so long as you also have a ladle. There's a cooler way to serve guests, however. Buy a spigot at a hardware store or on Amazon. Screw in the spigot near the bottom of the pumpkin, making sure it's tightly in there to prevent leakage.

# Dry Icing

No matter what your mom said, dry ice isn't dangerous per se, but it's not completely safe either. You don't want to grab it with your bare hands, and if you drink it you'll give your esophagus frostbites. Still, it's well worth using, because it's really cool-looking at a party.

The safest way to use it is to put a nice chunk in a bowl and then "float" it on top of your punch. The ballsier yet easier way is to just get some food-grade dry ice pellets and toss 'em on the top of your pumpkin punch. (Don't worry, they will have fully dissipated by the time they would have possibly worked their way to and through the spigot.) Dry ice will not just keep your punch chilled, a ghoulish smoke will waft out of the uncovered top of the pumpkin. People might even think it's the ghost of their alcoholic uncle Randy. Spooky!

# Skull-O Shots

Besides Cinco de Mayo there's another great Mexican holiday just thirsting for more liquid attention. It's a better holiday too—one that honors our loved ones who have passed, while celebrating the gathering of (still-living) family and friends. It's like sitting shiva with a whole lot more drunken dancing . . . and better drinks.

Meaghan Montagano, the beverage director at Brooklyn's Public Records, created this cheeky gelatin shot. She uses Cherry Coke Syrup and Dia de los Muertos skull molds, which can both be found online. However, if you can't find the syrup, make it yourself by boiling Cherry Coke over medium-high heat until it's reduced by half.

6 ounces mezcal

7 ounces Cherry Coke syrup

2 ounces Amaro Meletti

4 ounces fresh lime juice

1 packet unflavored Knox Gelatin

In a bowl, combine the mezcal, syrup, Amaro, and lime juice. In a separate bowl, combine the gelatin with 1½ ounces cold water and let sit for 5 to 10 minutes. Add 1½ ounces of warm water and whisk until combined. Add the liquor mixture into the gelatin, and stir to combine. Pour into individual molds and transfer them to the refrigerator until solid, about 4 hours.

To serve, pop the skulls out of their molds and transfer to a plate. If the shots are sticking to the mold, freeze them for an hour and try again.

# I Like Ike

Until just recently, there were a few states where you couldn't buy alcohol on Election Day. That was obviously ridiculous—before Prohibition our American voting system was built on boozing (to be fair, built on unscrupulous politicians buying votes with free booze). Luckily, things have changed for the better (kinda), and many folks have started hosting friends at their pads on election night to get liquored up and watch Wolf Blitzer tackle the returns.

A splendid accompaniment for calming everyone's nerves while waiting for those polls to close comes from San Francisco's Trick Dog. The drink first appeared there in the fall of 2016, on an election-themed menu meant to look like old-timey campaign buttons. Like this drink that recalls Dwight D. Eisenhower, none of the drinks referenced any of that year's candidates . . . which was probably a good thing.

7 ounces Plymouth Gin

2 ounces Noilly Prat Ambré Vermouth

4 ounces Raspberry Cucumber Shrub (opposite page)

1 ounce fresh lemon juice

4 egg whites

Orange peel (no pith)

Patriotic star sprinkles (red, white, and blue), for garnish (optional)

Combine the gin, vermouth, Raspberry Cucumber Shrub, lemon juice, and egg whites in a shaker (without ice) and do a dry shake. Add ice and shake hard.

Double strain into rocks glasses and add one large ice cube in each. Express the orange peel over the top and then discard. Garnish with the sprinkles.

# Raspberry Cucumber Shrub

Makes 25 ounces

3½ ounces raspberries

2 cups granulated sugar

6 ounces water

1 ounce diced cucumber,
plus 1 ounce cucumber juice

½ teaspoon kosher salt

¼ ounce dark chocolate

4¼ ounces sherry vinegar

In a saucepan, combine the raspberries and sugar and cook over medium-high heat until fully incorporated, about 10 minutes. Add the water, diced cucumber, salt, and dark chocolate. Bring to a simmer and remove from heat as soon as the chocolate is melted.

Once cooled, stir in the vinegar and cucumber juice. Strain into a container and refrigerate until ready to use or up to 2 weeks.

# Cranberry Punch

Thanksgiving is the consummate holiday for gluttony and bonhomie, a holiday where every single item on the menu is carefully thought-out, honed to please the majority of the family, then executed to perfection.

That is, except for the alcohol. Drinking on Turkey Day could best be described as "Every man for himself!" Mom has popped a bottle of Cab to sip on while cooking, dad is in the La-Z-Boy slugging Miller High Lifes, Uncle Tom has clearly gotten into . . . *something*, and you're stuck scrounging for anything decent in the liquor cabinet.

Well, if you're hosting the family, you need to seize the boozy reins and change things by making a special punch. One people can slowly sip on all day and all night, and which will assure all the leftover cranberry sauce doesn't go to waste either. That was the exact thinking behind this punch created by Billy Sunday's barman Stephanie Andrews.

1½ cups Old Tom gin

1½ cups Cocchi Americano

3 ounces Gran Classico Bitter

6 ounces fresh lemon juice

1 (750-milliliter) bottle sparkling wine

2½ cups Spiced Cranberry Syrup (page 21)

In a punch bowl, combine all the ingredients and stir together.

Insert a giant ice cube (see page 124), and have guests serve themselves.

# Making a Giant Ice Cube

While it is perfectly acceptable to make all the punches in this book with regular ice cubes that come out of your freezer, a slicker move is to make just one giant ice cube the size of the *entire* serving bowl. It won't only look cool, it will also prevent the punch from getting watery too quickly.

Camper English is the Internet's preeminent scholar on making cocktail ice, with nearly 100 articles about ice experiments on his website alcademics.com. For large format ice he recommends filling a small hard-sided cooler with water and then putting that in your freezer. Through a process called directional freezing, you will get a mostly crystal clear block of ice.

To remove it from the cooler, turn the cooler upside down on your kitchen counter and simply wait for it to slide out once it starts to melt. Preferably you will use a cooler the exact size of the cube you want for your punch bowl but, if not, you can cut it down by scoring lines and then hitting the block with an ice pick.

# The Gobbler Cocktail

Eating a gigantic, gluttonous, tryptophan-laden meal is always fun. The only problem is that you don't get to celebrate with friends. That's why the last few years have seen the emergence of "Friendsgiving." It's Thanksgiving but with the family you chose. It's usually held a weekend or two before the real Thanksgiving, and I wanted to give it a cocktail with a little more oomph, one that mimics the flavors in everyone's favorite leftovers sandwich, The Gobbler.

1½ cups Wild Turkey 101 Bourbon

4 ounces Laird's Applejack

4 ounces Spiced Cranberry Syrup (page 21)

24 dashes The Bitter Truth Original Celery Bitters

Stuffing cubes, for garnish (recipe follows)

In a pitcher, pre-batch by combining the bourbon, Applejack, and syrup, and stir.

To make individual drinks, pour 2½ ounces of the batch into a rocks glass and top with three dashes of bitters and one large ice cube. Garnish with a stuffing cube on a toothpick.

# Stuffing Cubes

Leftover stuffing

Olive oil, for drizzling

Leftover gravy

Preheat the oven to 400°F. Cut the stuffing into 1-inch cubes, place on a baking sheet, and drizzle with olive oil. Bake for 10 minutes, then flip over the cubes. Drizzle with the gravy and bake until dark brown and crisp.

# The Greyhound Sloshie

Guests of every major ski area across the world drink at the end of a day on the slopes. In most places in America it's basic beer or wine or simple mixed drinks. In Alpine resorts—where the practice began in the mid-1800s and the term "après-ski" first appeared by 1938—it has historically been schnapps. But in certain towns, unique après bevvies reign.

Jackson Hole, Wyoming, boasts its own version called the Sloshie, and despite the usually chilly temps, it's a frozen drink. Creekside Market serves the most popular one in town, essentially a frozen Greyhound they call The Hound.

Why should Jacksonites get to have all the fun? During the coldest time of the year, no matter how close you live to an actual chair lift, encourage your friends to bundle up (maybe even have a few bring their skis), come over, and slug some Sloshies.

1 cup vodka

4 cups fresh grapefruit juice

4 ounces Classic Simple Syrup (page 16), optional, if you would like it sweeter

Combine the all the ingredients with 2 cups of ice in a blender. Blend on high until you get a slushie-like texture. Pour into cups or insulated YETI mugs and serve.

# The Shotski

While no one is quite sure who invented it, plenty of people want to lay claim to it, and even more simply enjoy doing it. A "shotski" is, essentially, a group shot—several shot glasses are placed equally apart across the deck of a discarded downhill ski, allowing several folks to concurrently down a drink (or dump several shots all over themselves). While historically done in rowdy bars and ski lodges, increasingly people are enjoying the hijinks of slamming shotskis in the privacy of their own home. It certainly ups the party feel. As for acquiring a shotski, the bunny slope move is to order a commercial one online. The Blue Square move is to take an old ski and glue four or five shot glasses across its face. While the Double Black Diamond expert move is to do a shotski without the aid of glued-on shot glasses—that'll require some amazing synchronicity between the shotskiers.

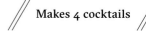

# A Repealing Idea

December 5, 1933, is a date any drinker should have seared into their memory. That, of course, was the day the 21st Amendment was passed and Prohibition finally came to an end. And many are still using the anniversary as an excuse to party hard.

Having your friends over and turning your apartment into a pseudo-speakeasy is an obvious choice—though, if Prohibition is over there's really no reason to "speak easy" anymore. You can probably skip dressing like a flapper and "tripping the lights fantastic" as well (though Harlem jazz playing on your Alexa might still be nice).

Most important is making sure everyone is sipping on this tipple, a modern riff on the Bee's Knees, made using distinctly Prohibition-era ingredients. The Old Forester 1920 Prohibition Style is designed to taste like "medicinal" bourbon which was *legally* distilled during those ugly thirteen years; while the Yuengling syrup honors the fact that D. G. Yuengling & Son sent a truckload of their eponymous beer to FDR literally on the day drinking was no longer prohibited.

1 cup Old Forester
1920 Prohibition Style
(or another bourbon)

3 ounces Yuengling
Beer Syrup (page 23)

3 ounces fresh lemon juice

12 dashes Fee Brothers
Cardamom Boker's Style
Cocktail Bitters

4 egg whites

Combine all the ingredients in a shaker (without ice) and do a dry shake. Add ice and shake hard.
Strain into chilled coupes and serve.

# Rowdy Toddy Piper

Getting people to come to your party is the easy part. Getting them to leave . . . well, that's another story, unless you have a cocktail that will do the trick. (No, it shouldn't be poisonous.)

Watershed Distillery beverage director Josh Gandee accidentally stumbled upon a cocktail fit for this Herculean task while toasting his large, extended family at his own wedding a few years back.

"The Rowdy Toddy Piper for me is the perfect way to say goodnight to friends after a raucous night," he explains. The Earl Grey adds "just enough of a calming runway without going into sleepy time territory." Just one of these hot toddy variants is enough to get everyone out of the house and off to their own beds.

And now you can finally clean up after everyone. Or, maybe save that for the morning.

4 ounces Underberg

4 ounces bourbon

2 ounces fresh lemon juice

1 ounce Demerara Syrup (page 18)

8 dashes The Bitter Truth Original Celery Bitters

2 cups hot Earl Grey tea

Lemon wheels adorned with cloves, for garnish

Combine all the ingredients in a heat-resistant pitcher and stir.

Divide among coffee mugs and garnish with the lemon wheels.

Now *that* was a party!

*Pictured on the following page*

# Acknowledgments

In the winter of 2018, a few months after my book *Hacking Whiskey* had been released, as the Dovetail Press team was wrapping up holiday promotion on the book, I started to realize: this is it. These people I'd talked to nearly every single day for over a year were about to be (mostly) out of my life. I kinda felt like I was being dumped. And I didn't want that. Then I had an idea: I should sell them another book! Luckily, it was around that time when this idea dropped in my lap.

I've thus had the joy of spending yet another year working with the dream team: editors Mura Dominko and Carlo Mantuano, photographer Scott Gordon Bleicher, photo retoucher Kate Anthony, designer Limor Evenhaim, production manager Chelsea Pinedo, prop stylist Christopher Spaulding, and food stylist Drew Aichele. Tessa Maffucci, Vicky Gu, and Cara McCabe who I constantly bother with texts telling her my "genius" ideas for marketing that I think she should pursue. And, of course, Josh Williams and Eric Prum.

I want to thank my wife, Betsy; daughter, Ellie; and cat, Hops; each of whom allows me to devote at least a third of our minimal fridge space to gigantic, boozy punches every few months or so. (Ask yourself if you'd let a three-year-old eggnog linger on your top shelf.)

Thanks to Cory and Traci for inspiration. I miss you guys already.

The bulk of this book was written at the Velvette Brew coffee shop in beautiful Park Slope, Brooklyn. This book can be accepted as my loyalty card and redeemed for one (1) free Americano.

## ABOUT THE AUTHOR

Aaron Goldfarb is a novelist and the author of *Hacking Whiskey: Smoking, Blending, Fat Washing, and Other Whiskey Experiments*. He writes about cocktails and drinking culture for *Esquire*, *PUNCH*, and *VinePair*, among other terrific websites and magazines. He lives in Park Slope, Brooklyn, with his wife, Betsy; daughter, Ellie; and Maine Coon cat, Hops. Hopefully you get to try his aged eggnog one day.